NATIONAL
GEOGRAPHIC

T0044741

Accidental Inventions

Rose Inserra

Contents

Introduction

What do chocolate chip cookies, matches, and Silly Putty® have in common? They are all things that were **invented** accidentally. The person who invented them was trying to do something else.

An inventor works to create something that solves a problem or addresses a need. But sometimes inventions happen by chance. Someone tries to do one thing, only to stumble upon a different good idea. Let's take a look at a few accidental inventions.

® Registered

When you see the ® symbol after a name, it means that the name of the product is **registered**. A registered name cannot be used on another product by other people.

Food

Many of the foods we eat have been invented by chance. Some of these foods have become very popular. Here are two stories about tasty treats that were made completely by accident.

Chocolate chip cookies are quick and easy to make.

Chocolate Chip Cookies

Can you imagine a world without chocolate chip cookies? They didn't exist before 1933 when Ruth Wakefield accidentally invented them. Wakefield was making chocolate cookies and ran out of baking chocolate. Rather than go to the store, she chopped a bar of chocolate into little pieces. She added the pieces to the cookie dough.

Wakefield got a surprise when she took the cookies out of the oven. The chocolate hadn't melted completely. There were little chips of chocolate in the cookies. The chocolate chip cookie was born. It is still many people's favorite cookie.

Ruth Wakefield

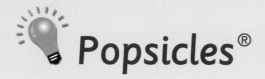

Popsicles®

Frank Epperson was just 11 years old when he invented a summer treat that we still love today. Back in 1905, people made soft drinks by blending a powdered mix with water. One cold winter's night, Epperson accidentally left the mix on his porch.

The next morning, Epperson found the mix was frozen solid. The stirring stick was standing straight up. He pulled the frozen drink out by the stick and licked it. It tasted great!

Frank Epperson

When Epperson grew up, he remembered his accidental invention. In 1923 he started the company that makes Popsicle® **brand** products. Children and adults have been enjoying these icy cold treats ever since.

Popsicles® are sold in many different flavors and colors.

Work and Home

Many everyday items were invented by accident. Others came about when people found a clever use for an invention that went wrong. Although none of these scientific inventions was planned, our lives would not be the same without them.

Lighting a fire is easy with a match.

Matches

Lighting a campfire would be much harder without the work of scientist John Walker. In 1826 he accidentally invented the match. After stirring a mixture of **chemicals**, Walker found that a hard little blob had dried on the tip of his wooden stick.

When Walker tried to remove the blob, it wouldn't come off. Walker rubbed the blob against the stone floor. He was amazed when the tip of the stick burst into flames! Walker had invented the match.

John Walker

Post-it® Notes

In 1968 Spencer Silver was trying to make a strong **adhesive**, or glue. He used the adhesive to glue two pieces of paper together. They stuck, but he could easily peel them apart without them tearing. What could anyone do with weak glue?

Arthur Fry

Arthur Fry had an idea. He worked at the same company as Silver. Fry used paper markers to keep his place in his book, but they kept falling out. Fry applied Silver's glue to the edge of one of his paper markers. He used it as a bookmark. The idea of the Post-it® Note was born.

Post-it® Notes have many uses.

Play

Many accidental inventions came about when people found a new use for something. Many toys were invented when someone thought of a new way to use something they already had.

Kids of all ages enjoy playing with a Slinky®.

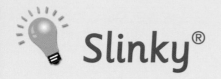 # Slinky®

We've all seen the Slinky®. It is a toy made out of an oversized spring. It is best known as the toy that "walks" down stairs. But who thought of it?

The Slinky® was invented by accident by a man named Richard James. He dropped a spring he was working on. To his surprise, the spring appeared to walk all by itself. He showed the spring's trick to his wife. She thought it would make a great toy. She named it Slinky®.

 Silly Putty®

This silly toy had a serious start. During World War II, **rubber** was needed to make airplane tires and soldiers' boots. So much rubber was needed that people couldn't collect enough rubber from rubber trees.

A man named James Wright tried to make rubber by mixing two chemicals together. The result was a glob of goo that bounced! Unfortunately, the goo was useless as a replacement for rubber.

James Wright

Silly Putty® is sold in plastic eggs.

Silly Putty® is easy to stretch into different shapes.

In 1949 a woman named Ruth Fallgatter thought the goo would make a fun toy. She hired a man named Peter Hodgson to see if it would sell. Hodgson found that people were very interested in the goo. He **packaged** the goo in plastic eggs and called it Silly Putty®. It was an instant success!

Glossary

adhesive   a substance, like glue, that makes things stick together

brand   the label that shows what company makes a product

chemical   a scientific ingredient

invent   to create something new

packaged   to wrap or present a product for sale

registered ®   a symbol that protects the name of a product so that it can't be used by others

rubber   a stretchy material made from the juice of a rubber tree